Epitaphs to Die For

The Poetry of Benchmarks

First Published: November 2016

Published by New World Books

Compiled by John Lane

A CIP catalogue record for this title is available from the British Library

ISBN 978-0-9934021-2-8

Printed and bound in Great Britain by
Witley Press, Hunstanton, Norfolk
www.witleypress.co.uk

Cover design by Chanticleer Studio, London SW11
www.chanticleerstudio.com

In Loving Memory

'Ready at last to set sail for the stars'

'We wrote your name in the sand, but the waves washed it away

We wrote your name in the sky, but the clouds blew it away

So we wrote your name in our hearts and forever it will stay'

'His was the fullest of lives, lived to the sound of laughter'

'And now, into the sunshine of God's love'

'If tears could build a stairway
And memories were a lane
We would walk right up to heaven
And bring you back again'

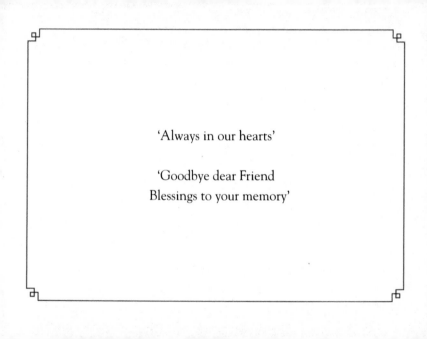

'Always in our hearts'

'Goodbye dear Friend
Blessings to your memory'

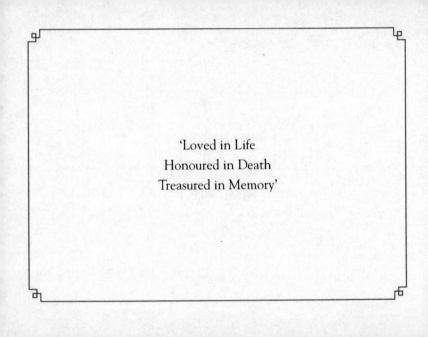

'Loved in Life
Honoured in Death
Treasured in Memory'

The greatest thing you'll ever learn
Is to love, and be loved in return'

'One day at a time – this is enough'

'Not, how did he die, but how did he live?
Not, what did he gain, but what did he give?'

'In all his life to any, come what might
He was a very perfect, gentle knight'

'Step into the sunshine, come out of the rain
For me dry your eyes, for me laugh again'

'Gone from sight but to memory dear'

'Not all the darkness in the world
Can put out the light of one small candle'

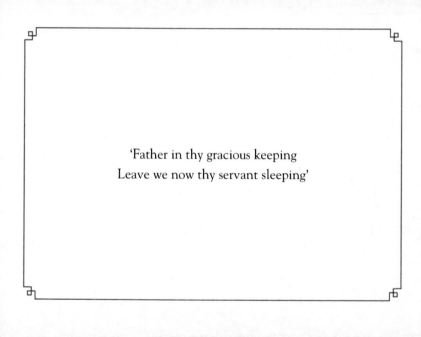

'Father in thy gracious keeping
Leave we now thy servant sleeping'

'Sunset and evening star
And one clear call for me!
And may there be no moaning of the bar,
When I put out to sea'

'May the winds be gentle, may the waves be calm'

'My dear husband now enjoys a heavenly berth
He is not lost but gone before
Safe home, safe home in port'

'God be in my heart and in my thinking
God be at my end and at my departing'

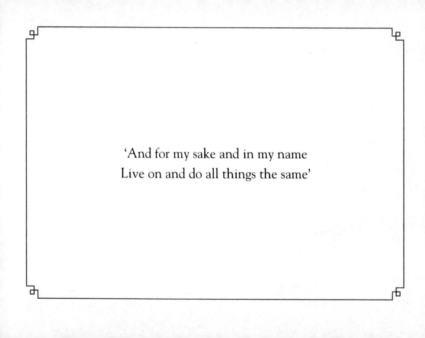

'And for my sake and in my name
Live on and do all things the same'

'The day thou gavest, Lord, is ended,
The darkness falls at thy behest'

'I said to the man who stood at the gate of the year
"Give me a light that I may tread safely into the unknown"'

'I have partaken long at the great banquet of life.
Now I hear the summoning trumpet calling'

'Lord, now lettest thou thy servant depart in peace'

'There is sadness in parting
But we take comfort in the hope that one day we will meet again'

'Tis a Gift to be Simple'

'In heaven – rest'

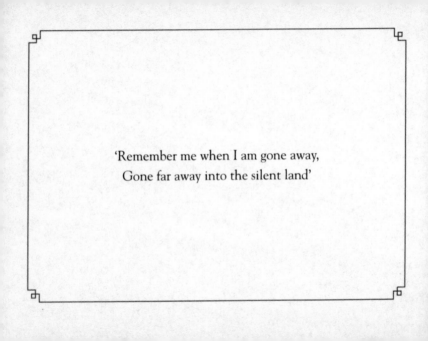

'Remember me when I am gone away,
Gone far away into the silent land'

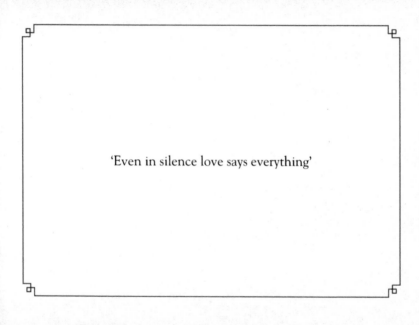

'Even in silence love says everything'

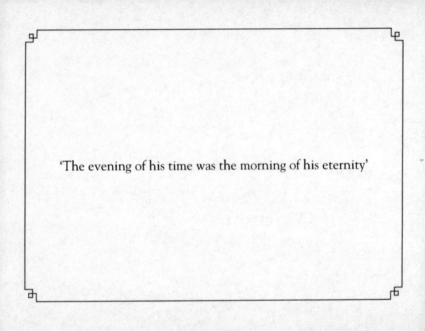

'The evening of his time was the morning of his eternity'

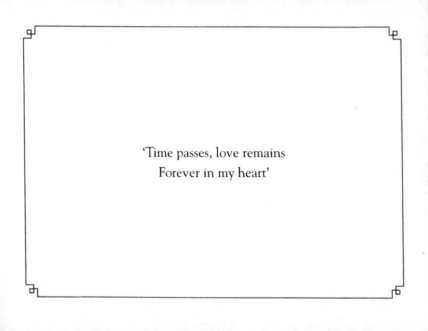

'Time passes, love remains
Forever in my heart'

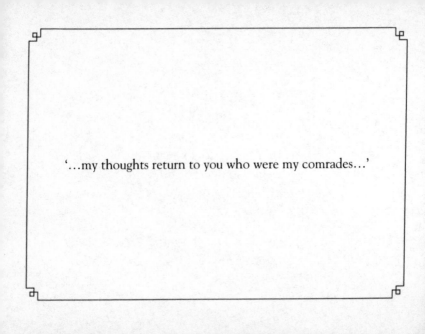

'…my thoughts return to you who were my comrades…'

'Even as age makes us forgetful,
Let us never forget our Comrades in Arms'

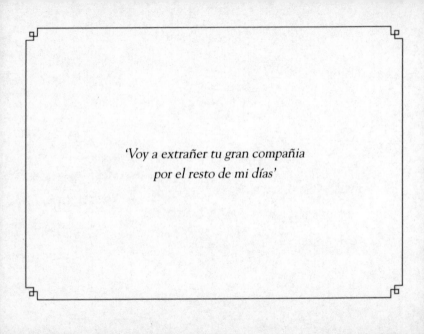

'Voy a extrañer tu gran compañia
por el resto de mi días'

'We were so fortunate to have walked
with one of God's angels in our time'

'Earth holds one gentle soul the less
And heaven one angel more'

'We shall pass through this world but once
Any good therefore that we can do
Or any kindness that we can show
To any human being
Let us do it now
Let us not defer or neglect it
For we shall not pass this way again'

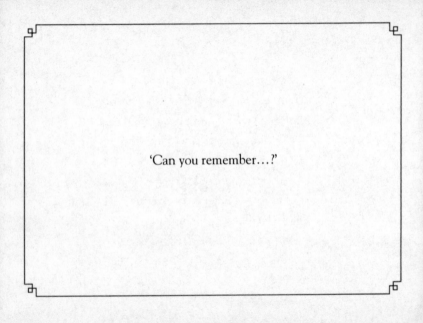

'Can you remember…?'

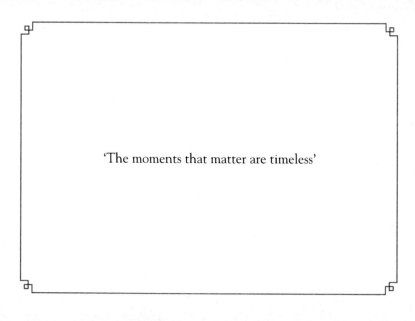

'The moments that matter are timeless'

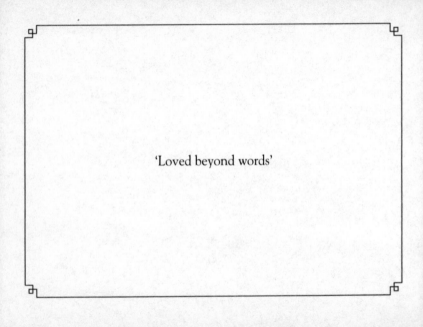

'Loved beyond words'

'Gone from us but not forgotten
Never shall thy memory fade
Sweetest thoughts will ever linger
Round the spot where thou art laid'

'Love knows not its own depth
Until the hour of separation'

'Farewell, dear darling of my soul.
We shall meet again, where the weary are at rest!'

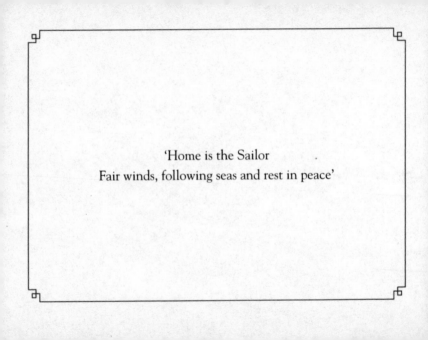

'Home is the Sailor
Fair winds, following seas and rest in peace'

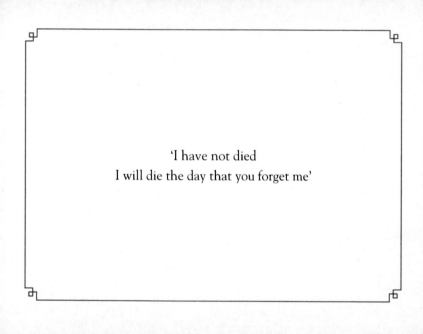

'I have not died
I will die the day that you forget me'

'If we are born to die,
Then we die to exist in the bosom of our creator'

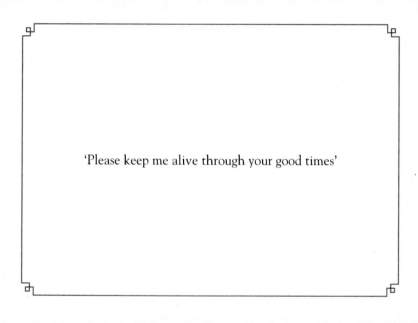

'Please keep me alive through your good times'

'We rejoice in your memory'

'You will always be with us
Shall we have another one here or move on?'

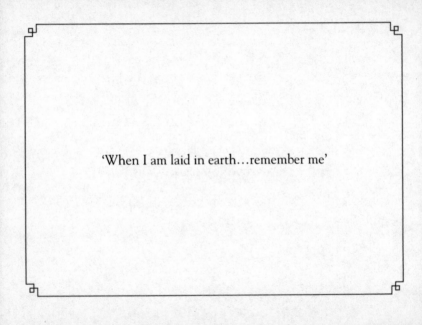

'When I am laid in earth…remember me'

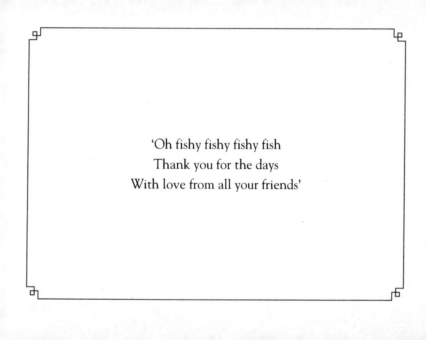

'Oh fishy fishy fishy fish
Thank you for the days
With love from all your friends'

'Her garden was a lifetime's work
It was a lifetime well spent
She lives on in the hearts of those who knew her'

'Adored friend whose love of life continues to inspire'

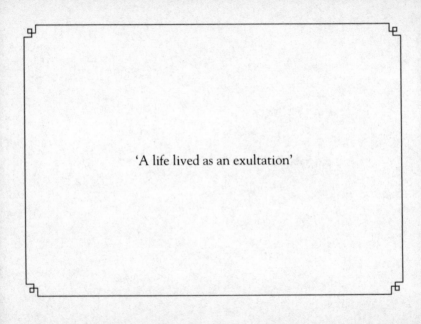

'A life lived as an exultation'

'You who have loved the evenings
And the great night sky
And the trees and the long grass blowing
You whose heart has sung
Think not with tears
That all has gone like a lost summer'

'Those whom we love never truly leave us.
They are forever in our hearts'

'Slowly, grief tires and sleeps, but never dies'

'He wandered much in the far and lonely places of the earth'

'Life is a journey
Travel it well'

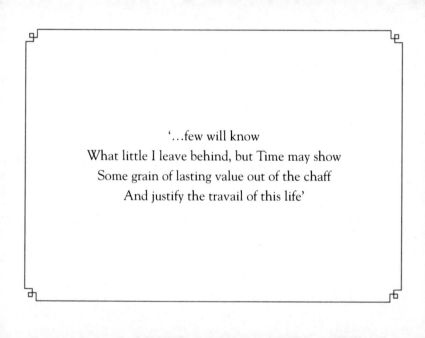

'…few will know
What little I leave behind, but Time may show
Some grain of lasting value out of the chaff
And justify the travail of this life'

'They are not long, the days of wine and roses'

'A farewell is necessary before we can meet again'

'Not heaven itself upon the past has power
What has been has been, and I have had my hour'

'Be to my virtues very kind
Be to my faults a little blind'

'He died as he lived –
With dignity, grace, clarity of purpose, fearlessness
And consummate consideration for others'

'And he would speed us onwards with a cheer
And wave from beyond the stars that all was well'

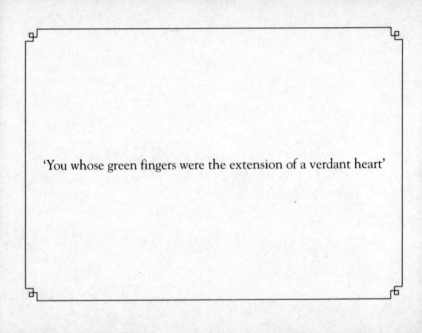

'You whose green fingers were the extension of a verdant heart'

'You are my dreams, you are my love, you are my life
I love you today, tomorrow and forever
Te quiero'

'Held forever safely in our hearts'

'For the sweet love remember'd, such wealth brings
That then I scorn to change my state with kings'

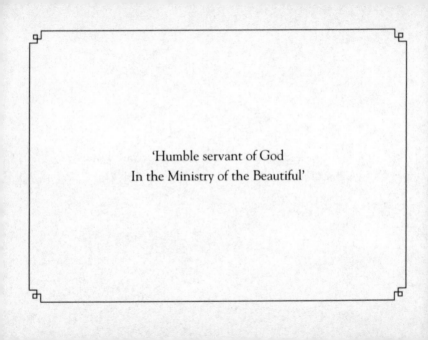

'Humble servant of God
In the Ministry of the Beautiful'

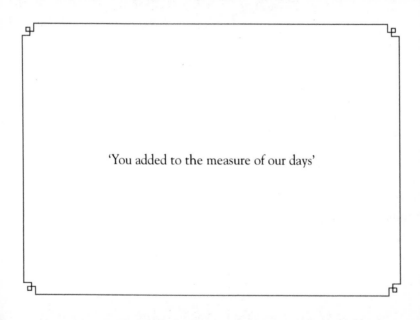

'You added to the measure of our days'

'Farewell, farewell my friend
It was beautiful as long as it lasted
The journey of our lives'

'So fall asleep, my love, loved by me…
…for I knew love, I was loved by thee'

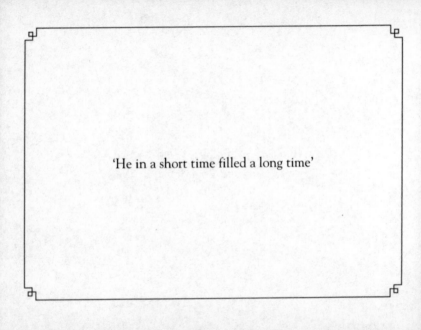

'He in a short time filled a long time'

'His race is run his work is done
May he obtain the prize
Be like the daily setting sun
Go down again to rise'

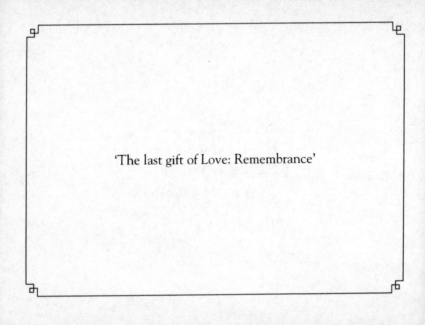

'The last gift of Love: Remembrance'

'When you live in the hearts of those you love
Remember then
You never die'

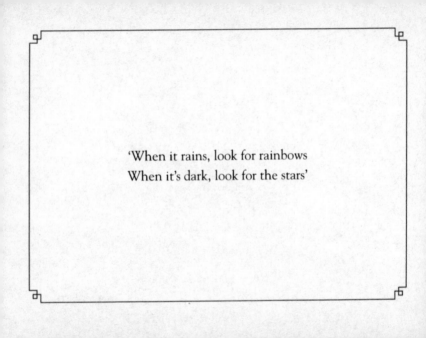

'When it rains, look for rainbows
When it's dark, look for the stars'

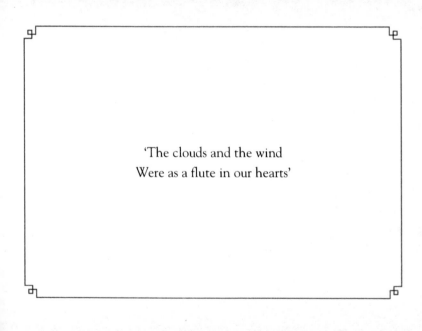

'The clouds and the wind
Were as a flute in our hearts'

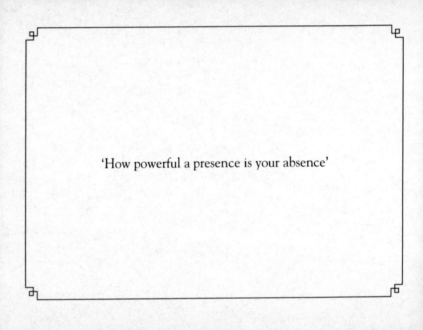

'How powerful a presence is your absence'

'May the road rise to meet you
May the wind be always at your back
May the sun shine warm upon your face
And may the rains fall softly upon your fields'

'For a time we acted on this stage
Sleep now, and say goodbye to the world'

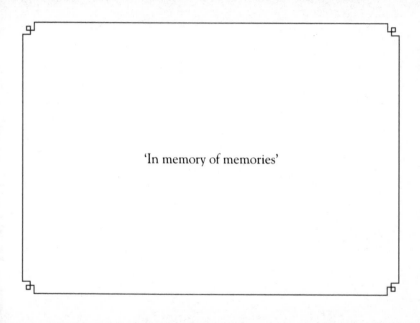

'In memory of memories'

'He was the master of his fate
He was the captain of his soul'

'Bon viveur, raconteur, tin collector extraordinaire – he was born to retire and went to Paradise by way of Kensal Green (and a hostelry or two!)'

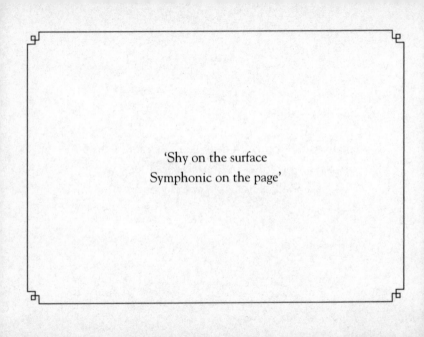

'Shy on the surface
Symphonic on the page'

'A fine writer who loved his commas
But now he has come to a full stop'

'May the wings of happiness be yours forever
For every Sunset there is a Sunrise'

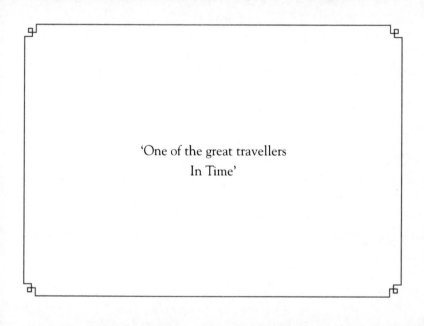

'One of the great travellers
In Time'

'If I should die and leave you here awhile,
Be not like others, sore and undone,
Who keep long vigils by the silent dust, and weep.
For my sake – turn again to life and smile
Nerving thy heart and trembling hand to do
Something to comfort other hearts than thine.
Complete those dear unfinished tasks of mine
And I, perchance, may therein comfort you.'

'Farewell, Sweet Prince –
May flights of angels sing you to your rest'

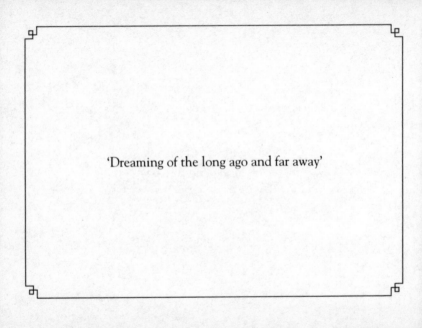

'Dreaming of the long ago and far away'

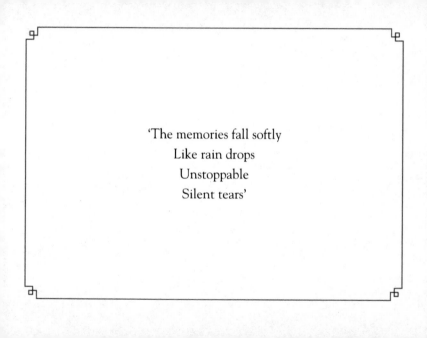

'The memories fall softly
Like rain drops
Unstoppable
Silent tears'

'These are our works
These works our souls display
Behold our works when we have passed away'

'And when the One Great Scorer comes
To write against your name
He marks not that you won or lost
But how you played the game'

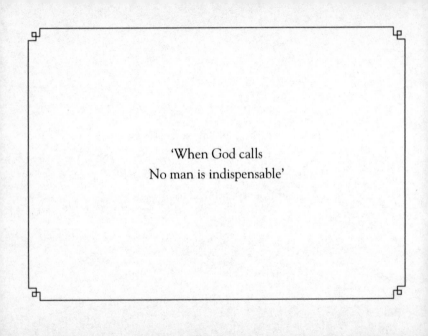

'When God calls
No man is indispensable'

'Rest in peace, and go well to your next place
The stars are not wanted now
Pack up the moon, dismantle the sun'

'Weep not for those whom the veil of the tomb
In life's early morning hath hid from our eyes'

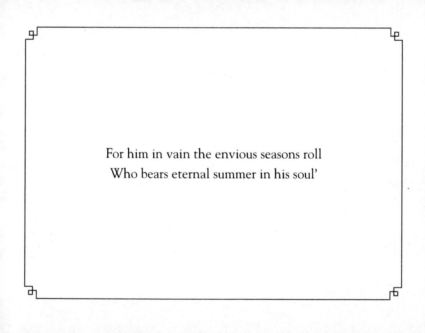

For him in vain the envious seasons roll
Who bears eternal summer in his soul'

'Hope…an anchor of the soul
Both sure and steadfast'

'Deep peace of the running wave to you
Deep peace of the flowing air to you
Deep peace of the quiet earth to you
Deep peace of the shining stars to you'

'Our common lot is a shared destiny'

'To lead our lives as though they will go on forever
Is the most common human vanity'

The Cemetery

'Nobody has a name in this place.
Today we are but an atom of dust
The democracy of the dead'

'A strong wind has blown the pages of my life
There is only one left
The end of a book'

'…never send to know for whom the bell tolls…'